1694-1778 Voltaire, Thomas Francklin

Matilda: A tragedy

As it is performed at the Theatre-Royal, in Drury-Lane

1694-1778 Voltaire, Thomas Francklin

Matilda: A tragedy
 As it is performed at the Theatre-Royal, in Drury-Lane

ISBN/EAN: 9783337038861

Printed in Europe, USA, Canada, Australia, Japan

Cover: Foto ©ninafisch / pixelio.de

More available books at **www.hansebooks.com**

MATILDA

A

TRAGEDY.

As it is performed at the

THEATRE - ROYAL,

IN

DRURY-LANE.

By the AUTHOR of the EARL OF WARWICK.

DUBLIN:

Printed for J. Exshaw, W. Sleater, J. Potts,
D. Chamberlaine, J. Williams, W. Wilson,
J. Sheppard, J. A. Husband, R. Moncrieffe,
R. Marchbank, T. Walker, C. Jenkin, and
J. Hillary. M. DCC. LXXV.

DEDICATION.

TO THE PUBLIC.

SIR,

PERMIT me to return you my unfeigned
thanks for your kind reception of this TRA-
GEDY on the ftage, and to requeft the con-
tinuance of your favour to it in the clofet. It
would be the higheft ingratitude in me to forget
the only patron I ever had the good fortune to
meet with, by whofe powerful affiftance I have
been enabled to defeat the combined forces of
envy, malice and detraction. I muft at the
fame time fairly confefs, my victory over the
enemy was owing, I believe, as many other
victories have been, more to the art and
prowefs of my OFFICERS than to any ex-
traordinary merit of my own. To the firft
in command, Mifs YOUNGE, I have infinite
obligations, which I fhall always gratefully
acknowledge, tho' I may never have it in my
power to repay them; nor can the fkill and
conduct of my generals, REDDISH, SMITH,
and PALMER, be fufficiently admired. To
your patronage and protection I moft heartily
and fincerely recommend them: If I have
been the happy inftrument of giving them a
favourable opportunity of rifing in YOUR
efteem, it will give me the greateft fatisfaction.
YOU can beft diftinguifh their merit, and
YOU alone are able to reward it.

I am, Sir, your much obliged,

And devoted humble Servant, -

A 2 *The Author.*

Dramatis Personæ.

M E N.

MORCAR,	}	*Earl of Mercia,*	{ Mr. REDDISH.
EDWIN,	}	*Earl of Northumberland,*	{ Mr. SMITH.
SIWARD,	}	*Morcar's friend,*	{ Mr. PALMER.

OFFICERS, &c.

W O M E N.

MATILDA,	}	*A prisoner in the camp of Morcar,*	{ Miss YOUNGE.
BERTHA,	}	*Her friend,*	{ Miss PLATT.

SCENE, MORCAR's *Camp, and the Environs near* NOTTINGHAM.

PROLOGUE.

WRITTEN BY A FRIEND.

SPOKEN BY Mr. SMITH.

A Tragic Tale, from Norman William's Age,
Simple, and unadorn'd, attempts the Stage.
Our silly Bard, more simple than his Tale,
Thinks on your polish'd Manners to prevail;
What in those barb'rous Days were counted Crimes,
Are Slips of course in these enlighten'd Times:
Let not your Ancestors too rude appear,
Though firm in Friendship, and in Love sincere.
Love then like Glory did each Heart inflame,
Beauty was Virtue, and to win it, Fame.
Now Lovers lose their Mistresses with Grace,
As at New-Market they would lose a Race,
Where, if in Hopes they seem a little cross'd,
'Tis for the Money of the Match that's lost.
When Tilts and Tournaments call'd forth the Brave,
The Fame of spotless Innocence to save,
Each gallant Knight preferr'd his Love to Life,
For then the greatest Blessing was a Wife:
To prove their Chastity the dauntless Fair
Would walk through Flames, nor singe a single Hair;
Nay, some so chaste, so cold to all Desire,
Not only 'scap'd it, they put out the Fire!
But now no Heroes die for Love's sweet Passion,
And fiery Trials are quite out of Fashion.
Ye Sons of Frailty——you whom Rage devours,
For you this Night the Muse exerts her Pow'rs;
With crimson Hands, pale Cheeks, and blood-shot Eyes;
She bids the Furies in their Terrors rise!

A 3   In

PROLOGUE.

In Valour's Breaſt their Scorpion Stings they dart,
Firſt fire the Brain, and then corrupt the Heart.
But what avails all Virtue ! Paſſion's Guſt,
Like Whirlwinds, drive it from the Heart like Duſt;
When Reaſon dawns, well may Repentance mourn
Love, Friendſhip, Duty, by the Roots up-torn.
To ſooth this fatal Vice, the Flatterer tells
In ſtormy Minds how warmeſt Friendſhip dwells ; .
The Tree whoſe ſheltering Arms ſpread kindly round,
If Light'ning-ſtruck, lies blaſted on the Ground ;
In vain will Merits paſt Indulgence claim,
One Moment's Raſhneſs blaſts whole Years of Fame.

EPILOGUE.

EPILOGUE.

By the AUTHOR of the TRAGEDY.

SPOKEN BY Miss YOUNGE.

HA! ha! poor Creature! how you trembling stand!
Come to the Bar, Sir, and hold up your Hand;
You won't — by Council then you'd have it done,
And I must plead your Cause—well, get you gone.
　　　　　　　　[Coming forward to the Audience.
Now for the great Tribunal of Old Drury;
Are you all sworn there—Gem'men of the Jury?
Good Men, and true, I hope—stay, let me see,-
Amongst you all he challenges—but three.
Physicians, Lawyers, Parsons he admits,
Beaux, Ladies, Courtiers, Maccaronies, Cits, }
And only scratches—Critics, News-writers, and Wits.

The Critic first we banish from our Session,
Death is his Trade, and Damning—his Profession;
Disqualify'd—because, to say no further,
Butchers are never heard in Case of Murther.

Next we disclaim th' Artificers of News,
Who live by Fibs, and flourish by Abuse;
They must condemn, or lose their daily Bread;
If they don't cut, and slash—they're never read;
Like fabled Giants here they roam for Food,
And Fe! Fa! Fum! snuff up an Author's Blood;
In the next Ledger hang him up to roast,
Or tear him Piece-meal in—the Morning-Post.

To Wits we last except, and 'bove all other,
The Hero of our Tale—a Rival Brother!

A 4

EPILOGUE.

As Rogues, just 'scap'd the Gallows, join the Shrieves,
Turn Hangmen, and tuck up their Fellow-Thieves;
So Bards condemn'd, exert the Critic's Skill,
And execute their Brethren of the Quill!
If like their own, indeed, the Brat should die,
They'll gladly join to write—its Elegy;
But if the Child is strong, and like to live,
That is a Crime they never can forgive.

From such let English Juries still be free,
Our Author here appeals to your Decree,
The Public is—a Court of Equity.
If he has shock'd your Taste, your Sense, or Reason,
Or against Nature guilty been of Treason,
Off with his Head;—but if with honest Art,
His well-meant Scenes have touch'd the feeling Heart;
If they have rais'd your Pity, wak'd your Fears,
Or sweetly have " beguil'd you of your Tears,"
Let venial Errors your Indulgence claim,
Your Voice his Triumph, your Applause his Fame.

Speak by your Foreman—what says Goodman Pit?
Will you condemn the Prisoner, or acquit?
Your Verdict, Sirs, Not Guilty—if you please—
You smile—Acquitted—hope you'll pay his Fees.

MATILDA:

A TRAGEDY. *

ACT I.

SCENE, MATILDA's *Tent, with a view of the distant country.*

MATILDA, BERTHA.

MATILDA.

I Thank thee, gentle Bertha, for thy goodness ;
If aught cou'd footh the anguish of my foul,
Or raife it from the horrors of defpair
To hope and joy, 'twou'd be thy gen'rous friendfhip:
But I am funk fo deep in mifery,
That comfort cannot reach me.

A 5   Bert.

---

* *The reader will meet with some lines which, to shorten*
the scenes, were omitted in the reprefentation.

Bert.   Talk not thus,
My sweet Matilda; innocence, like thine,
Must be the care of all-directing heav'n.
Already hath the interposing hand
Of Providence redeem'd thee from the rage
Of savage war, and shelter'd thee within
This calm asylum.   Mercia's potent Earl,
The noble Morcar, will protect thy virtues,
And, if I err not, wishes but to share
His conquests with thee.

    Matil.   O, my friend, oft times
The flow'ry path that tempts our wand'ring steps
But leads to mis'ry ; what thou fondly deem'st
My soul's best comfort, is its bitt'rest woe.
Earl Morcar loves me.   To the gen'rous mind
The heaviest debt is that of gratitude,
When 'tis not in our power to repay it.

    Bert. Oft have I heard thee say, to him thou ow'st
Thy honour and thy life.

    Matil.   I told thee truth.
Beneath my father's hospitable roof,
I spent my earlier happier days in peace
And safety : When the Norman conqueror came,
Discord, thou know'st, soon lit her fatal torch,
And spread destruction o'er this wretched land.
The loyal Ranulph flew to William's aid,
And left me to a faithful peasant's care,
Who liv'd, sequester'd in the fertile plains
Of rich Northumbria : There awhile I dwelt
In sweet retirement, when the savage Malcolm
Rush'd on our borders.

    Bert.   I remember well
The melancholy hour.   Confusion rag'd
On ev'ry side, and desolation spread
Its terrors round us.   How did'st thou escape ?

                             Matil.

Matil. A crew of defp'rate ruffians feiz'd upon me,
A helplefs prey: For, O! he was not there,
Who beft cou'd have defended his Matilda.
Then had I fall'n a wretched facrifice
To brutal rage, and lawlefs violence,
Had not the gen'rous Morcar interpos'd
To fave me: Tho' he join'd the guilty caufe
Of foul rebellion, yet his foul abhor'd
Such violation. At his awful voice
The furly ruffians left me, and retir'd.
He bore me, half expiring in his arms,
Back to his tent; with ev'ry kind attention
There ftrove to footh my grie's, and promis'd, foon
As fit occafion offer'd, to reftore me
To my afflicted father.
    Bert.   Something fure
Was due to gen'rous Morcar for his aid,
So timely given.
    Matil.   No doubt: But mark what follow'd.
In my deliverer too foon I found
An ardent lover, fighing at my feet.
    Bert. And what is there the proudeft of our fex
Cou'd wifh for mo ? To be the envy'd bride
Of noble Morcar, firft of England's peers,
In fame and fortune.
    Matil.   Never truft my Bertha,
To outward fliew. 'Tis not the fmiles of fortune,
The pomp of wealth, or fplendor of a court,
Can make us happy. In the mind alone,
Refts folid joy, and true felicity,
Which I can never tafte: For, O, my friend!
A fecret forrow weighs upon my heart.
    Bert. Then pour it in the bofom of thy friend;
Let me partake it with thee.
                        Matil.

Matil.   Gen'rous maid!
Know then, for nought will I conceal from thee,
I honour Mercia's Earl, revere his virtues,
And wish I cou'd repay him with myself;
But, blushing, I acknowledge it, the heart
His vows solicit, is not mine to give.

   Bert. Has then some happier youth————

   Matil.   Another time
I'll tell thee all the story of our loves.
But, O, my Bertha! did'st thou know to whom
My virgin faith is plighted, thou wou'd say
I am indeed unhappy.

   Bert.   Cou'd Matilda
Bestow the treasure of her heart on one
Unworthy of her choice?

   Matil.   Unworthy! No.
I glory in my passion for the best,
The loveliest of his sex. O! he was all
That bounteous nature, prodigal of charms,
Did on her choicest fav'rite e'er bestow.
His graceful form and sweet deportment spoke
The fairer beauties of his kindred soul,
Where ev'ry grace and ev'ry virtue shine.
But thou wilt tremble, Bertha, when I tell thee,
He is Earl Morcar's—brother.

   Bert.   Ha! his brother!
The noble Edwin? Often have I heard
My father————

   Matil.   Did Lord Edrick know him then?

   Bert. He knew his virtues, and his fame in arms,
And often wou'd lament the dire effects
Of civil discord, that cou'd thus dissolve
The ties of nature, and of brethren make
The bitt'rest foes. If right I learn, Lord Edwin

Is

Is William's firmeſt friend, and ſtill ſupports
His royal maſter.

   Matil.   Yes, my Bertha, there
I ſtill find comfort: Edwin ne'er was ſtain'd
As Morcar is, with foul diſloyalty,
But ſtands betwixt his ſov'reign and the rage
Of rebel multitudes, to guard his throne.
If nobly fighting in his country's cauſe,
My hero falls, I ſhall not weep alone ;
The king he lov'd and honour'd, will lament him,
And grateful England mix her tears with mine.

   Bert. And doth Earl Morcar know of Edwin's love ?

   Matil. O, no ! I would not for a thouſand worlds
He ſhou'd ſuſpeſt it, leſt his fiery ſoul
Shou'd catch th' alarm, and kindle to a flame
That might deſtroy us all.

   Bert.   I know his warmth
And vehemence of temper, unreſtrain'd
By law, and ſpurning at the royal pow'r
Which he contemns, he rules deſpotic here.

   Matil. Alas ! how man from man, and brother oft
From brother differs ! Edwin's tender paſſion
Is ſoft and gentle as the balmy breath
Of vernal zephyrs ; whilſt the ſavage north,
That curls the angry ocean into ſtorms,
Is a faint image of Earl Morcar's love :
'Tis rage, 'tis fury all. When laſt we met
He knit his angry brow, and frown'd ſevere
Upon me ; then, with wild diſtraſted look,
Bade me beware of trifling with his paſſion,
He wou'd not brook it—trembling I retired,
And bath'd my couch in tears.

   Bert.   Unhappy maid !
But time, that ſoftens ev'ry human woe,
Will bring ſome bleſt event, and lighten thine.

                                Matil.

Matil. Alas ! thou know'ft not what it is to love.
Haply thy tender heart hath never felt
The tortures of that foul-bewitching paffion.
Its joys are fweet and poignant, but its pangs
Are exquifite, as I have known too well :
For, O ! my Bertha, fince the fatal hour
When Edwin left me, never hath fweet peace,
That us'd to dwell with all its comforts here,
E'er deigned to vifit this afflicted breaft.

Bert. Too plain, alas ! I read thy forrows grief ;
Sits in fad triumph on thy faded cheek,
And half obfcures the luftre of thy beauties.

Matil. Talk not of beauty, 'tis our fex's bane,
And leads but to deftruction. I abhor
The fatal gift. O ! would it had pleas'd heav'n
To brand my homely features with the mark
Of foul deformity, or let me pafs
Unknown, and undiftinguifh'd from the herd
Of vulgar forms, fave by the partial eye
Of my lov'd Edwin ; then had I been bleft
With charms unenvy'd, and a guiltlefs love.

Bert. Where is thy Edwin now ?

Matil.   Alas I know not.
'Tis now three years fince laft thefe eyes beheld
Their deareft object. In that humble vale,
Whence, as I told thee, Malcolm's fury drove me,
There firft we met. O ! how I cherifh ftill
The fond remembrance ! There we firft exchang'd
Our mutual vows, the day of happinefs
Was fixt ; it came, and in a few fhort hours
He had been made indiffolubly mine,
When fortune, envious of our happinefs
And William's danger, call'd him to the field.

Bert. And fince that parting have ye never met ?

                                        Matil.

Matil. O never, Bertha, never but in thought.
Imagination, kind anticipator
Of love's pleasures, brings us oft' together.
Oft' as I fit within my lonely tent,
And caft my wifhful eyes o'er yonder plain,
In ev'ry paffing traveller I ftrive
To trace his image, hear his lovely voice
In ev'ry found, and fain wou'd flatter me
Edwin ftill lives, ftill loves his loft Matilda.

    Bert. Who knows but fate, propitious to thy love,
May guide him hither.

    Matil.   Gracious heav'n forbid !
Confider, Bertha, if the chance of war
Shou'd this way lead him, he muft come in arms
Againft his brother: Oh ! 'tis horrible
To think on. Shou'd they meet, and Edwin fall,
What fhall fupport me ? And if vict'ry fmiles
Upon my love, how dear will be the purchafe
By Morcar's blood ! Then muft I lofe my friend,
My guardian, my protector—ev'ry way
Matilda muft be wretched.

    Bert.   Is there ought
In Bertha's pow'r

    Matil.   Wilt thou difpatch, my friend
Some trufty meffenger with thefe ?—Away.

                      (gives her letters.
I'll meet thee in my tent—farewel.   [*Exit Berth.*

    Matil. (alone)   Mean time
One hope remains, the gen'rous Siward—he
Might fave me ftill. His fympathetic heart
Can feel for the afflicted.—I have heard,
(Such is the magic pow'r of facred friendfhip)
When the impetuous Morcar fcatters fear
And terror round him, he, and he alone

                              Can

Can stem the rapid torrent of his passion,
And bend him, tho' reluctant, to his will;
And see, in happy hour, he comes this way.
Now fortune, be propitious! if there be,
As I have heard, an eloquence in grief,
And those can most perfuade, who are most wretched,
I shall not pass unpitied.

Enter SIWARD.

 Siw.   Ha! in tears,
Matilda! What new grief, what cruel foe
To innocence and beauty, thus cou'd vex
Thy gentle spirit?
 Matil.   Canst thou ask the cause,
When thou behold'st me still in shameful bonds.
A wretched captive, friendlefs and forlorn,
Without one ray of hope to sooth my sorrows.
 Siw. Can she, whose beauteous form, and fair de-
Charm ev'ry eye, and conquer ev'ry heart,   meanor,
Can she be wretched? can she want a friend,
Whom Siward honours, and whom Morcar loves?
O! if thou knew'st with what unceasing ardor,
What unexampled tendernefs and truth,
He dotes upon thee, sure thou might'st be wrought
At least to pity.
 Matil.   Urge no more, my Lord,
Th' ungrateful subject; but too well I know
How much thy friend deserves, how much, alas,
I owe him!—If it be Earl Morcar's wish
To make me happy, why am I detain'd
A pris'ner here? Spite of his solemn promise
He would restore me to my royal master,
Or send me back to the defiring arms
Of the afflicted Ranulph, who in tears

Of bitt'reft anguifh, mourns his long-loft daughter?
Surely, my lord, it ill becomes a foldier
To forfeit thus his honour and his word.

Siw. I own it; yet the caufe pleads ftrongly for him.
If by thy own too powerful charms mifled,
He deviates from the paths of rigid honour,
Matilda might forgive. Thou know'ft he lives
But in thy fmiles; his love-enchanted foul
Hangs on thofe beauties he would wifh to keep
For ever in his fight.

Matil,   Indulgent heav'n
Keep me for ever from it! O, my Lord!
If e'er thy heart with gen'rous pity glow'd
For the diftrefs'd; if e'er thy honeft zeal
Cou'd boaft an influence o'er the man you love;
O! now exert thy pow'r, affift, direct,
And fave thy friend from ruin and Matilda.
There are, my Lord, who moft offend, where moft
They wifh to pleafe. Such often is the fate
Of thy unhappy friend, when he pours forth
His ardent foul in vows of tend'reft paffion;
'Tis with fuch rude and boift'rous violence
As fuits but ill the hero or the lover.

Siw. I know his weaknefs, know his follies all,
And feel 'em but too well: He loves with tranfport,
And hates with fury. Warm'd with fierce defire,
Or ftrong refentment, his impetuous foul
Is hurried on, till reafon quits her feat,
And paffion takes the loofely-flowing rein;
Then all is rage, confufion, and defpair.
And yet, when cool reflection hath remov'd
The veil of error, he will weep his faults
With fuch a fweet contrition, as wou'd melt
The hardeft heart to pity and forgivenefs.
O! he has virtues that may well atone

For

For all his venial rafhnefs, that deferve
A fov'reign's love, and claim a nation's praife;
Virtues that merit happinefs and thee.
Why wilt thou thus defpife my noble friend?
His birth and fortune, with the rank he bears
Amongft the firft of England's peers, will raife thee
As far above thy fex, in wealth and pow'r,
As now thou art in beauty.

    Matil.   O, my Lord!
'Tis not the pride, the luxury of life,
The fplendid robe and glitt'ring gem, that knits
The lafting bonds of mutual happinefs:
Where manners differ, where affections jarr,
And will not kindly mix together, where
The fweet harmonious concord of the mind
Is wanting, all is mifery and woe.

    Siw. By heav'n, thou plead'ft thy own and virtue's
With fuch bewitching eloquence, the more   {caufe,
Thy heart, alarm'd by diffidence, ftill urges
Againft this union with my friend, the more
I wifh to fee him bleft with worth like thine.

    Matil. My Lord, it muft not be; for grant him all
The fair perfections you already fee,
And I fou'd wifh to find, there is a bar
That muft for ever difunite us——Born
Of Norman race, and from my earlieft years
Attach'd to William's caufe; I love my king
And wifh my country's peace: That king, my Lord,
Whom Morcar wifhes to dethrone; that peace
Which he deftroys: Had he an angel's form,
With all the virtues that adorn his fex,
With all the riches fortune can beftow,
I wou'd not wed a traitor.

    Siw. Call not his errors by fo harfh a name;
He has been deeply wrong'd, and fouls like his,

                            Muft

Muſt feel the wounds of honour, and reſent them.
Alas! with thee I weep my country's fate,
Nay wiſh, perhaps, as well to William's cauſe,
And England's peace, as can the loyal daughter
Of gallant Ranulph, and wou'd, therefore, joy
To ſee Matilda lend a gracious ear
To Morcar's ſuit. Thy reconciling charms
Might ſooth his troubled ſoul, might heal the wounds
Of bleeding England, and unite us all
In one bright chain of harmony and love.
The gallant Edwin too——
 Matil.   Ha! what of him?
Know'ſt thou that noble youth?
 Siw.   So many years
Have paſt ſince laſt we met, by diff'rent views,
And our unhappy feuds, ſo long divided,
I ſhould not recollect him; but report
Speaks loudly of his virtues. He, no doubt,
If yet he lives——
 Matil.   Yet lives!—Why, what, my Lord?
 Siw. You ſeem much mov'd.
 Matil.   Forgive me, but whene'er
This ſad idea riſes to my mind,
Of brother againſt brother arm'd, my ſoul
Recoils with horror.
 Siw.   'Tis a dreadful thought;
Wou'd I cou'd heal that cruel breach! but then
Thou might'ſt do much, the taſk is left for thee.
 Matil. For me? Alas! it is not in my pow'r.
 Siw. In thine, and thine alone. O think, Matilda!
How great thy glory, and how great thy praiſe,
To be the bleſſed inſtrument of peace;
The band of union 'twixt contending brothers.
Thou ſee'ſt them now, like two deſcending floods,
Whoſe rapid torrents meeting, half o'erwhelm

                                        The

The neighb'ring plains: Thy gentle voice might ftill
The angry waves, and bid their waters flow
In one united ftream, to blefs the land.

Matil. That flatt'ring thought beams comfort on my
Amidft my forrows; bear me witnefs, heav'n! (foul,
Cou'd poor Matilda be the happy means
Of reconcilement: Cou'd thefe eyes behold
The noble youths embracing, and embrac'd
In the firm cords of amity and love:
O! it would make me ample recompence
For all my griefs, nor would I more complain,
But reft me in the filent grave, well pleas'd
To think, at laft, I had not liv'd in vain.

Siw. Cherifh that virtuous thought, illuftrious maid,
And let me hope my friend may ftill be happy.

Matil. I wifh it from my foul: But fee, my Lord,
Earl Morcar comes this way, with hafty fteps,
Acrofs the lawn. I muft retire: Farewel!
You'll not forget my humble fuit.

Siw.   O! no,
I will do all that lovelieft innocence
And worth like thine, deferve. Farewel: Mean time
Remember, Siward's every wifh, the blifs
Of Morcar, Edwin's life, the public peace,
And England's welfare, all depend—on thee.

                                    [*Exit Matilda.*

Siw. (alone) There's no alternative but this; my friend
Muft quit Matilda, or defert the caufe
We've rafhly promis'd to fupport—Perhaps
The laft were beft—both fhall be try'd—he comes.

Enter MORCAR.

Morc.   O, Siward! was not that
The fair Matilda, whom you parted from?

                                    Siw.

Siw. It was.

More. What fays fhe? the dear, cruel maid!
Is fhe ftill deaf? inexorable ftill?

Siw. You muft not think of her.

More. What fay'ft thou, Siward?
Not think of her!

Siw. No. Root her from thy heart,
And gaze no more. I blufh to fee my friend
So loft to honour: Is it for a man,
On whom the fate of England may depend,
To quit the dang'rous poft, where duty calls,
And all the bus'nefs of the war, to figh
And whine in corners for a captive woman?
Refume the hero, Morcar, and fubdue
This idle paffion.

More. Talk not thus of love,
The great refiner of the human heart,
The fource of all that's great, of all that's good;
Of joy, of pleafure—If it be a weaknefs,
It is a weaknefs which the beft have felt;
I wou'd not wifh to be a ftranger to it.

Siw. Let me entreat thee, if thou valueft life,
Or fame, or honour, quit Matilda.

More. Yes:
I thank you for your counfel. 'Tis th' advice
Of cold unfeeling wifdom, kindly meant
To make me prudent, and to leave me wretched:
But thus it is, that proud exulting health
Is ever ready to prefcribe a cure
For pain and ficknefs which it never knew.

Siw. There too thou err'ft; for I have known its joys
And forrows too. In early life I loft
The partner of my foul. E'er fince that hour
I bade adieu to love, and taught my foul
To offer her devotions at the fhrine

of

Of facred friendfhip; there *my* vows are paid:
Morcar beft knows the idol of my worfhip.

   Morc. I know and love thee for it: But O! my friend,
I cannot force this tyrant from my breaft;
E'en now I feel her here, fhe fits enthron'd,
Within the foldings of my heart, and he
Who tears her thence muft draw the life-blood from me.
My morning flumbers, and my midnight dreams,
Are haunted by Matilda.

   Siw.   To be thus
The flave of one that fcorns thee, O! 'tis bafe,
Mean and unworthy of thee.

   Morc.   •   I will bear
That fcorn no longer: Thou haft rous'd me, Siward;
I will enjoy the glorious prize; fhe's mine,
By right of conqueft mine. I will affert
A victor's claim, and force her to be happy.

   Siw. That muft not be. It ill becomes the man
Who takes up arms againft a tyrant's pow'r,
T' adopt a tyrant's maxims; force and love
Are terms that never can be reconcil'd.
You will not, muft not do it.

   Morc.   Muft not! who
Shall dare oppofe me!

   Siw.   Honour, confcience, love,
The fenfe of fhame, your virtue, and your friend.
Whilft I have life, or pow'r, I will not fee
Matilda wrong'd.

   Morc.   You are her champion then
It feems, her favour'd, happy friend, perhaps
Her fond admirer too. Ill-fated Morcar!
I fee it but too well. I'm loft, abandon'd;
Alike betray'd by friendfhip and by love.
I thank you, Sir, you have perform'd your office,
And merit your reward.

                     Siw.

Siw.   Unkind reproach !
Did I for this defert my Sov'reign's caufe,
My peaceful home, and all its joys, to ferve
Ungrateful Morcar ? Why did I rebel ?
The haughty William never injur'd me.
For thee alone I fought, for thee I conquer'd ;
And, but for thee, long fince I had employ'd
My gallant foldiers to a nobler purpofe,
Than loit'ring thus in idle camp to hear
A love-fick tale, and footh a mad man's phrenzy.
   Morc. You could ? Away, and leave me then<
       With-draw
Your boafted aid, and bid Northumbria's fons
Bend to the tyrant's yoke, whilft I alone
Defend the caufe of freedom, and my country.
Here let us part. Remove your loiterers,
And join th' ufurper.
   Siw.   Mark the diff'rence now
Betwixt blind paffion and undaunted friendfhip :
You are impatient of the keen reproof,
Becaufe you merit : I can bear it all,
Becaufe I've not deferv'd it.

Enter an OFFICER.

   Offic.   Good, my Lords,
Forgive this rough intrufion, but the danger,
I truft, will plead my pardon. As I watch'd
From yonder tow'r, a dufky cloud appear'd,
As if from diftant troops advancing, foon
I faw their armour glitter in the fun ;
With rapid motion they approach'd ; each moment
We muft expect them here.
                           Siw.

Siw.   Why, let 'em come,
Already I have order'd fit difpofal
Of all our little force. Away, good Ofmond,
Be filent and be ready.   (*Exit Officer.*
       Now, my friend,
Thou art as welcome to thy Siward's breaft,
As dear as ever.—When the man I love,
Walks in the paths of error, I reprove him
With honeft freedom ; but when danger comes
Upon him, I forget his faults, and flee
With all a lover's ardour to his refcue ;
His forrows and his wants alone remember'd,
And all his follies buried in oblivion.

Morc. Thou haft difarmed me now. This pierces more
Than all the bitter poifon of reproach,
Which thou haft pour'd upon me. O! 'twas treafon
Againft the facred majefty of friendfhip,
To doubt thy honour, or fufpect thy virtue.
Thou wilt forgive: But when the wounded mind
Is torn with paffion, ev'ry touch is pain ;
You fhould not probe fo deeply.

Siw.   'Twas my duty.
But come, no more of that. The foe advances.
If we fucceed, as my prophetic foul
Foretels we fhall—I have fome comfort for you—
If not, we'll borrow courage from defpair,
And die like men. Thou ftand'ft upon the rock
Of danger, and the yawning precipice
Opens before us ; I will fnatch thee from it,
Or leap the gulph, and perifh with my friend.

The End of the Firft Act.

A C T · II.

SCENE, *a Fortrefs belonging to* MORCAR.

EDWIN *alone (in chains.)*

EDWIN.

IT is the will of heav'n, and muft be done.
The hard-fought field is loft, and here I am
A pris'ner in my brother's camp : alas!
That fortune thus fhou'd guide me to a foe
Whom moft I wifh'd to fhun! We little thought
The troops by Morcar led, had this way bent
Their ill-directed courfe : but Providence
Hath fo ordain'd, perhaps, to heal the wounds
Of civil difcord. O! unhappy Edwin,
For what art thou referv'd ? No matter what:
Since fate depriv'd me of my dear Matilda,
Whom I for three long years have fought in vain ;
Life hath been irkfome to me : this, perchance,
May end it——For, who knows if nature yet
May live within the conqu'ror's breaft, to plead
A brother's pardon ? Yet he knows me not,
But foon he muft——Ha! who comes here? Earl
        Siward !——
The fecond in command, to whom, o'erpower'd
By circling foes, and fainting with my wounds,
I yielded up my fword. If fame fay true,
He bears a mind too great to look with fcorn
On the opprefs'd, or triumph o'er misfortune.

B   *Enter*

Enter SIWARD.

Siw. Stranger, whoe'er thou art, be comforted;
Thy fate hath thrown thee into noble hands,
Who know thy merit. May I afk thy name?
  Edw. I am a poor abandon'd wretch, the fport
Of fortune; one whofe leaft affliction is
To be a captive, and from ev'ry eye
Wou'd wifh to hide the ftory of my fate :
Too foon my name and forrows will be known.
  Siw. Refpect is ever due to mifery :
.I will not urge thee further; all I hope,
'That gen'rous pity could afford to footh
·Calamity like thine, by my command
.Hath been extended to thee. Heie awhile
You muft remain a pris'ner, but ere long
I hope to greet thee by a fairer name,
And rank thee as our friend.
  Edw.   Your gen'rous orders
..Have been obey'd, and I acknowledge it
With grateful heart   May I not afk the fate
Of him who fought fo nobly by my fide,
That brave old man.
  Siw.,   The gallant Ranulph—
  Edw.   Yes;
My fellow captive.
  Siw.   He is fafe and free.
  Edw. Ha! free! Thank heav'n!
  Siw.   The gen'rous Morcar, urg'd
By my entreaties, pardon'd and releas'd him,
Tho' much our foldiers murmur'd, and demanded
His life and your's ; a facrifice, they faid,
Due to the manes of their flaughter'd friends ;
But mercy has prevail'd.

Edw.

Edw.   What e'er becomes
Of an unhappy wanderer, like me,
For your kind treatment of the aged Ranulph,
Accept my thanks ; it was a precious boon ;
Morcar may find me not unworthy of it.
To day I am his captive, but to-morrow
May fee me his deliverer : for know
My royal mafter, the victorious William,
With eagle fwiftnefs, foon will follow me
With twenty times your force. As this fhall prove
Or true, or falfe, fo deal with me ; remember
I warn'd you of it.

Siw.   And remember thou
That I with joy receive the welcome news :
Welcome to me, for I am William's friend.

Edw. Thou can'ft not then be mine, or England's foe:
With fuch a heart as thine, fo nobly form'd
To feel for the afflicted, fatisfy'd,
For thou feem'ft, of William's royal right,
What cou'd engage thee in this foul revolt,
This bafe rebellion ?

Siw.   What but the great bond
Of kindred fouls, inviolable friendfhip !
The only folid blifs on this fide heav'n,
That doubles all the joys of human life,
And, by dividing, leffens ev'ry woe.

Edw. Who knows but this day's fad event may prove
The happy means to heal a nation's wounds,
And footh our jarring factions into peace ?

Siw. Had Morcar thought with me, long fince that end
Had been obtain'd ; but Morcar is—

Edw.   Inexorable.
So I have heard, and therefore little hope
To change his nature. O ! cou'd he be wrought
To fweet oblivion of his wrongs ; to bury

B 2   His

His deep refentment : Mine fhou'd be the tafk,
A tafk, heav'n knows, I wou'd with joy perform,
To reconcile offended majefty :
To foften all his errors, plead his pardon,
And give my fov'reign one brave foldier more.

Siw. When next we meet I truft it fhall be fo :
Mean time, let me prepare him for the change ;
Retire a while—ere long we'll fend for thee,
For ev'ry moment I expect him here :
Thy freedom and thy happinefs fhall be
My firft concern, for thou haft well deferv'd it.

Edw. Farewel. Be quick in your refolves ; the time
Requires it ; and be wife ere 'tis too late.

　　　　　　　　　　　　　　　　[*Exit Edwin.*

　　　　　S I W A R'D.　　(*alone*)

I hope we fhall. This well-tim'd victory,
If rightly us'd, may fmooth our way to peace.
Now, Morcar, all thy happinefs depends
Upon thyfelf alone. Now, friendfhip, raife
Thy pow'rful voice, and force him to be happy.
He will, he muft—he comes—

　　　　　　　Enter M O R C A R.

Siw.　　　　My conqu'ror, welcome !
Mort. Thrice welcome to my arms, my noble Siward,
At length we meet in joy, the day is ours ;
Thanks to thy friendly aid.
Siw.　　　　　We muft not boaft ;
'Twas hardly purchas'd, and has coft us dear :
You follow'd 'em too clofe.
Morc.　　　　　I own 'twas rafh ;
My youthful ardor urg'd the keen purfuit
Too far ; and but for thee I had been loft.

　　　　　　　　　　　　　　　　　　In

In war, thy arm protects me, and in peace,
Thy councils guide. O! how shall I return
Thy goodness? Thou wert born to save thy friend.
  Siw. Away, I'll not be thank'd. I've done my duty,
And if thou think'st thyself indebted for it,
Repay me not with flatt'ry, but with love.
E'er since my soul with thine, congenial met
In social bands, and mark'd thee for her own,
Thy int'reft and thy happiness have been
My first ambition; and when thou art bleft
With all thy soul can wish for, Siward then,
And then alone, will have his full reward.
  Morc. O, unexampled faithfulness and truth!
But say, my Siward, is our loss so great?
  Siw. The flow'r of half our troops. But 'tis not now
A time to weep, for I have glorious tidings,
That much imports thy happiness.
  Morc.   Ha! what?
  Siw. Know that amongst our captives I have ta'en
A noble prize, will make us full amends
For ev'ry loss—the gallant Raoulph.
  Morc.   Ha!
Matilda's father! then I'm satisfy'd.
The wily chief! by heav'n he shall repay me
For her unkindness: Give him to my rage,
To my resentment, to my injur'd love.
Where is he, Siward?
  Siw.   I have set him free.
  Morc. Ha! free! Thy ill-tim'd mercy hath betray'd
Our cause. The tyrant wou'd have ransom'd him
With half his kingdom.
  Siw.   Still thy rapid passions
O'erpow'r thy reason. What if it shou'd serve
A better purpose; smooth thy paths to bliss,
And gain Matilda for thee!
          B 3   *Morc.*

More.   O, my friend!
My Siward, do not flatter me: By heav'n,
Her kind confent wou'd give my ravifh'd foul
More true and heart-felt happinefs, than cou'd
A thoufand vict'ries o'er the proud ufurper.

   Siw. Know then, I gave him liberty and life
On thefe conditions—That he fhou'd withdraw
His pow'rs from William's aid, and never more
Affift his caufe; the time wou'd come, I told him,
That he fhou'd know to whom he ow'd the boon,
And how he might repay it.

   More.   That was kind,
Indeed, my Siward, that was like a friend.
O! thou reviv'ft my drooping heart; but tell me,
Did my Matilda, let me call her mine,
Did fhe acknowledge, did fhe thank thee for it?

   Siw. O! I affum'd no merit; but to thee,
And to thy gen'rous, unexampled love,
Did I attribute all. She figh'd, and wept,
Pour'd forth a thoufand bleffings on thy head——

   More. And doft thou think, my Siward, that one ray
Of hope remains?

   Siw.   The clouds already vanifh,
The profpect brightens round thee; hafte and feize
The lucky moment. When the gen'rous mind
Is footh'd by obligation, fooh it opens
To the mild dictates of humanity,
And foftens into fympathy and love.

   More. O, Siward! cou'd'ft thou teach me but to win
That lovely maid——

   Siw.   The tafk is half perform'd
Already, and my friend fhall foon be blefs'd.
One thing, and one alone, remains to fix
Her doub'ful heart, if yet a doubt remains.

Morc. O! name it, Siward; if 'tis in the pow'r
Of wealth to purchafe, or of victory.
In the fair field of glory to acquire,
It fhall not long be wanting.

    Siw. It requires
No price, but fuch as Morcar well can pay;
No vict'ry, but the vict'ry o'er thyfelf,
And thy own paffions—Give up thy refentment,
Make peace with William, and Matilda's thine.

    Morc. Matilda mine! and muft I purchafe her
At the dear price of honour? with the lofs
Of all my foul holds dear, my country's welfare?
My word——

    Siw. Away! whilft prudence warranted;
Our honeft zeal, I was the firft to aid
Thy juft revenge; but valour ill-advi.'d,
And ill-exerted in a hopelefs caufe,
Degen'rate into rafhnefs. You miftake
The pride of honour, for the pride of virtue.

    Morc. And wou'd'ft thou have me bend beneath the
Of ignominious flav'ry, quit the caufe   {yoke
Of heav'n-born freedom, and betray my friends?

    Siw. I'd have thee juft and happy—We have been
Succefsful, let us now be generous,
Whilft we have fomething to beftow; nor wait
Till fickle fortune from our brow fhall tear
The blafted wreath, and leave us nought to give.
Too long already have we facrific'd
At proud ambition's altar, to revenge;
Now let us offer at the fhrine of peace,
And facrifice——

    Morc. To love, and to Matilda;.
It fhall be fo—the ftruggle's paft—away,
My Siward, hafte, and tell her, I obey;
Her laws, her king, her mafter fhall be mine;:

    I have

I have no will but hers, and in her eyes
Will read my duty—Yet a moment stay,
What will my brave companions of the war,
My fellow foldiers fay ? Will they approve
This unexpected change ?

   Siw.   I know them firm
In their obedience, and refolv'd to act
As you command—But I will fee 'em ftrait,
And urge fuch pow'rful reafons as may beft
Secure them to our purpofe. Fare thee well.

   Morc. Siward, thy kind anticipating care
Prevents my ev'ry wifh—But fay, my friend,
Where is the gallant chief, whom we fubdu'd,
Who fought fo hardly, and fo nobly fell ?

   Siw. In yonder tent, a wretched pris'ner ftill,
He counts the tedious hours; a heavy gloom
Sits on his brow, as if fome deep-felt forrow
Opprefs'd his noble mind—We muft releafe him.

   Morc. Thou know'ft, my Siward, thrice we had o'er-
His troops, and thrice his fingle valour turn'd (pow'r'd
The fortune of the day : Since firft I trod
The paths of glory, ne'er did I behold
Such deeds of valour wrought by mortal hand;
I almoft envy'd, though I conquer'd him.
He wore his beaver up, nor could I trace
His features, but he bears a noble form :
Know'ft thou his quality or name ?

   Siw.   Not yet;
He feems induftrious to conceal them both
From ev'ry eye.

   Morc.   Some deity protects him,
As its peculiar care, for as I rais'd
My fword againft him, whether the foft paffion
That triumphs o'er me, had unmann'd my foul,
I know not; but, bereft of all its pow'r,

                                    My

My nervele*s* arm dropp'd ineffe&ual down,
And let him 'fcape me.
   Siw.   'Tis moft true, I faw
And wonder'd at it. When you left the field,
With defp'rate rage he ru*fh*'d intrepid on,
And feem'd to court his fate, till circling foes.
Compell'd him to refign, and yield his fword.
   Morc. Away. I burn with ardor to forgive,
To free, and to embrace him: fly, my Siward.
Let him approach, he cou'd not wifh to meet
In happier hour, the mafter of his fate,
For now, methinks, I cou'd be reconcil'd
To ev'ry foe. Away, my Siward, hafte
And fend him to me.
   Siw.   Treat him like a friend,
He may be ufeful. Such diftinguifh'd merit
Muft have its influence, he commands, no doubt,
The royal ear, and may procure fuch terms
As William may with honour yield, and we
Without a blufh accept.   *(Exit. Siward.*
   Morc. (alone)   Farewel. And now
How ftands the great account ? Can I acquit
Myfelf, or fhall I be condemn'd before
Thy great tribunal, all-repaying juftice ?
But fair Matilda wipes out ev'ry ftain,
'Tis fhe commands me to forgive, and fhe
Muft be obey'd ; I'm not the firft apoftate
From honour's caufe the tyrant love has made.
My friend too urg'd the change——
          (Guards bring in Edwin chained.
          He's here—Strike off
Thofe ignominious chains—he has deferv'd
A better fate.   *(Guards unchain him.*
   Stranger, whoe'er thou art,   *(turning to Edwin*
Thy gallant bearing in th' unequal conflict,

For we had twice thy numbers, hath endear'd
A foldier to a foldier.   Vulgar minds
To their own party, and the narrow limits
Of partial friendfhip, meanly may confine
Their admiration ; but the brave will fee,
And feeing, praife the virtues of a foe.
    Edw. *(afide.)* O, pow'rful nature, how thou work'ft
             within me!
    Morc. Still filent! ftill conceal'd! perchance thou
Knowing thy rank and name, I might recal   (fear'ft,
My promis'd pardon ; but be confident,
For by that facred honour, which I hold
Dearer than life, I promife here to free,
And to protect thee : did'ft thou hide from me
My deadlieft foe: Shou'd William's felf appear
Before me, he who hath fo deeply wrong'd me,
So long oppos'd : Nay, fhou'd I hear the voice
Of that advent'rous, rafh, mifguided youth,
Whom yet I cannot hate—my cruel brother,.
I cou'd forgive him.
    Edw. *(difcovering himfelf.)* Then behold him here.
    Morc. Edwin! Amazement! By what wond'rous
Myfterious Providence, do'ft thou unfold   (means,
Thy fecret purpofes ? I little thought
When laft we met, what heav'n-protected victim
Efcap'd my fword.
    Edw.   .   With horror I recal.
The dreadful circumftance. Throughout the battle
I knew, and carefully avoided thee.
    Morc. O, Edwin ! how, on this propitious day,
Have vict'ry, fame and friendfhip, fortune, love
And nature, all confpir'd to make me bleft!
We have been foes too long—Of that no more.
My Edwin, welcome ! Once more to thy arms
Receive a brother.

Edw.-

Edw.   Yet a moment ſtay:
By nature touch'd the ſame accordant ſtring
That vibrates on thy heart now beats on mine;
But honour, and the duty which I owe
The beſt of kings, reſtrain the fond embrace
I wiſh to ſhare, and bid me aſk, if yet
In Morcar I behold my fov'reign's foe.
If it be ſo, take back thy proffer'd freedom,.
Take back my forfeit life: I wou'd not wiſh
To be indebted for it to—a traitor.

Morc Perhaps I may deſerve a better name ;,
Perhaps I may be chang'd.

Edw.   I hope thou art;;
For this I came, for this I yielded to thee,
To tell thee William's ſtrength is ev'ry hour
Increaſing: if thou mean'ſt to make thy peace,
Now is the criſis——

Morc.   Edwin, ſtop, nor urge
Such mean unworthy motives as alone
Cou'd thwart my purpoſe. Morcar cannot fear,
But Morcar can be gen'rous : for know,
Before I ſaw thee here I had reſolv'd
To ſheath my ſword and be the conqu'ror's friend ;
For O ! there is a cauſe——.

Edw.   Whate'er the cauſe,
Th' effect is glorious. Now thou art again
My brother. Here, let us once more unite
The long-diſſever'd cord.   *(They embrace.*

Morc.   And never more
May blind reſentment, faction, party, rage,
Envy, or jealous fear, diſſolve the tye !
And now, my Edwin, bluſhing, I confeſs,
Not to thy tender care for Morcar's ſafety,
To friendſhip's council, or to reaſon's voice,
Owe we this wiſh'd for change. A female hand
Directs and wills it.   *Edw.*

Edw.   Ha!, a woman!

Morc.   · Yes,
If fuch I ought to call, that form divine,
Which triumphs here, who rules my ev'ry thought,
My ev'ry action guides. In yonder tent
A beauteous captive dwells, who hath enflav'd
Her conqu'ror: She demands the facrifice;
She wou'd not give her hand to William's foe,
And therefore, only, Morqar is his friend.

Edw. I cou'd have wifh'd that this important change
Were to the hero, not the lover, due.

Morc. I am above deceit, and own my weaknefs;
But thou fhalt fee her—Yes, my Edwin, thou
Shalt bear the welcome tidings to my love.
Thy prefence will bear witnefs to the change;
Thy freedom, and the joyful news thou bring'ft
Of our bleft union, will confirm it to her.
Wilt thou, my Edwin—

Edw.   Do not afk me what.
I muft refufe. I wou'd do much to ferve
A friend and brother; but, a tafk of joy
Ill fuits a foul opprefs'd with griefs like mine.
O! I cou'd tell thee—but 'twou'd be unkind,
When thou art ent'ring on the paths of blifs,
To ftop thee with my melancholy tale.

Morc. What e'er thy griefs, I pity, and hereafter
May find the means to leffen, or remove them;
Mean time this tender office may divert
Thy forrows; nay, if thou deny'ft me, Edwin,
I fhall not think our union is fincere.

Edw. Then be it fo.

Morc.   I'll fend a trufty flave
That fhall conduct thee to her. Soon I mean
To follow thee—away—begone and profper.

                              But,

But, O, my brother! if thou haſt a heart
That is not ſteel'd with ſtoic apathy
Againſt the magic of all conqu'ring love,
Beware of beauty's pow'r; for ſhe has charms
Wou'd melt the frozen breaſt of hoary age,
Or draw the lonely hermit from his cell
To gaze upon her.

 Edw.   Know, thy fears are vain;
For long, long ſince, by honor's ſacred tyes,
United to the lovelieſt of her ſex,
Edwin, like Morçar, is to one alone
Devoted, and *my* heart is fix'd as thine.

 Morc. Then I am bleſt. Thy ſympathetic ſoul,
With warmer feelings, ſhall expreſs *my* paſſion,
Wak'd by the fond remembrance of thy *own*.

Go then, thy kind returning friendſhip prove,
Go, plead with all the eloquence of love;
And as thou do'ſt thy brother's anguiſh tell,
Still on thy lips may ſoft perſuaſion dwell!
Urge my fond ſuit with energy divine,
Nor ceaſe till thou haſt made the lovely captive mine.

The End of the Second Act.

A C T

A C T III.

Matilda Bertha.

Matilda.

O, Bertha! I have had fuch frightful dreams,
They harrow'd up my foul.

   Bert.   It is the work
Of bufy fancy in thy troubled mind ;
Give it no heed.

   Matil.   O! it was more, much more
Than fancy ever form'd ; 'twas real all ;
It haunts me ftill, and ev'ry circumftance
Is now before me ; but I'll tell thee all.
Scarce had I clos'd my eyes, to feek that reft
Which long had been a ftranger, when methought
Alone I wander'd thro' a mazy wood,
Befet with thorns and briars on ev'ry fide ;
The mournful image of my wretched ftate :
When, from a winding walk, the beauteous form
Of my lov'd Edwin, feem'd to glide acrofs,
And ran with hafte to meet me : But, behold !
A tyger rufh'd between, and feiz'd upon him :
I fhriek'd aloud.

   Bert.   'Twas terrible.

   Matil.   But mark
What follow'd ; for a gleam of light broke in,
And fav'd me from defpair : When 'crofs the glade

                     A gen'rous

A gen'rous lyon, as with pity mov'd
At the unequal conflict, darted forth
And sprung with vengeance on the spotted beast,
Who turn'd with fury on his nat'ral foe,
And loos'd my Edwin; he escap'd, and fled:
I wak'd in agonies.
  Bert.   Be comforted;
The dream presages good: Some gen'rous friend
Shall save him from the perils of the war,
And give him to thy longing arms again.
  Matil. O, never, never!

     Enter an OFFICER.

  Officer.   Noble lady, one
From William's camp, by Morcar's orders sent,
Wou'd crave a minute's conference, and says
He bears some news that may be welcome.
  Matil.   Ha!
From William's camp! O, flatt'ring hope! who knows
But he may bring some tidings of my love!
Tidings, perhaps, I may not wish to hear.
Perhaps he comes to speak of Edwin's death;
Or Edwin's falshood—Be it as it may,
I cannot be more wretched than I am.
Conduct him hither.   (*Exit Officer.*
      O, my flutt'ring heart!
Look yonder! how imagination forms
What most we wish for; see, he comes—It is,
It is my Edwin—Save me, Bertha! O!
       (*as he enters she faints.*

     Enter EDWIN.

  Edw. What do I see? Matilda here! she faints!
           Am.

Am I deferted then ? abandon'd, loft,
Betray'd by her I love ? She breathes, fhe lives !
But not for me—for Morcar; for my brother.

MATILDA, *(to Bertha)*

Where is he ? O ! it was delufion all;
The form deceiv'd me.   Had it been my love,.
He wou'd have flown with rapture to me—See
He ftands far off, and will not look upon me.
   Edw.   I dare not.
   Matil.   Is it thus we meet again ?
Is this the kind, the tender, faithful Edwin ?
   Edw. Art thou Matilda ? Speak ; for I am loft
In wild aftonifhment.   It cannot be.
In Morcar's camp !, Is this the lovely captive.
That I fhou'd meet ?
   Matil.   All-feeing heav'n,.
Bear witnefs for me : If, from that fad hour
When laft we parted, this devoted heart
Hath ever wander'd, ever caft one thought,
Or form'd a wifh for any blifs but thee,
Defpife me, Edwin ; flight me, caft me off
To infamy and fhame.
   Edw.   I muft, I muft
Believe thee ; Yet, 'tis ftrange—when thou fhalt know
From whom I came, and what my errand here.
Thou wilt not call me cruel or unkind,
When I fhall tell thee I am come to claim
Another's right, O ! heav'n, another's right
To my Matilda ; to requeft thy hand
For Morcar.
   Matil.   For thy brother !
   Edw.   Yes, ev'n now
We parted.—Here he told me I fhould meet
A beauteous captive ; little did I think

It was Matilda, whom he long had woo'd;
Whofe gen'rous heart, he hop'd, wou'd now accept
A convert made to loyalty by love;
She only waited for that bleſt event,
With mutual ardour to return his paſſion.
Can it be thus? Alas! thy prefence here
Confirms it but too well.

Matil.   Appearance oft,
By ſtrange events and caufelefs jealoufy,
Confounds the guilty with the innocent.
But fure my Edwin's noble mind difdains
To cheriſh low fufpicion; 'tis a vice
Abhorrent to thy nature, and Matilda
Will never practice it on thee. True love
Knows not diſtruſt, or diffidence, but reſts
On its own faith fecure, and hopes to meet
The truth it merits.

Edw.   Can this be the voice
Of falſhood?—Can thofe lips?————

Matil.   Miſtaken man!
Cou'dſt thou e'er credit the delufive tale?
Cou'dſt thou believe I had fo foon forgot
My plighted faith? But fince I am fufpected,
Return, and bear this anfwer back to Morcar.
Firſt fay, I thank him for the choice he made
Of thee to be the herald of his love:
For what is there Matilda can refufe,
That Edwin could requeſt?

Edw.   O! that recals
A thoufand tender thoughts————

Matil.   Go tell him too,
What e'er I raſhly promis'd but to gain
A few ſhort moments, to preferve my king,
And fave a father's life, I never meant
To feign a paſſion which I cou'd not feel;

                                             Foſ

For I was deftin'd to another's arms ;
To one, who now regardlefs of his vows
To poor Matilda, after three long years
Of cruel abfence from her, comes at laft
To doubt her honour, and fufpect her love.

Edw. O! never, never, Sooner will I doubt
The pow'rs of nature, and believe thefe eyes
Can mifinterpret ev'ry object here,
Than think thee falfe. O! take me to thy arms
And bury all my doubts.—Can'ft thou forgive
The jealous warmth of agonizing paffion ?

Matil. I can : I muft. But fay, to what bleft chance
Am I indebted for this happy moment ?

Edw. The chance of war. I am a pris'ner here,
And but for thee——

Matil. When I fhall tell thee all
That I have fuffer'd fince we parted laft
Thou wilt not blame, but pity poor Matilda.
Mean while be calm ; it is not now a time
For idle doubts and vifionary fears
When real dangers threat. I fee already,
By thy imperfect tale, what mifery
Muft foon await us, when the fiery Earl
Shall know this ftrange event.

Edw. And wherefore know it
Why not conceal our paffion, till fome means
Of freedom offer ?

Matil. I abhor the thought.
No, Edwin, no. The crifis of our fate
Approaches. Never let us ftain our loves
With crooked fraud and bafe diffimulation.
Hark! did'ft thou hear a voice in yonder grove?
Siward in conf'rence with the haughty Earl ;
Behold them—fee—they part—and Morcar haftes

With

With quick impatient ſtep, to know his fate.
Now ſummon all thy pow'rs.

   Edw.   I am prepar'd.
He comes : a few ſhort minutes will determine
Whether Matilda plays the hypocrite,
Or is deſerving of her Edwin's love.

Enter MORCAR.

   Morc. At length I hope Matilda's ſatisfy'd.
Edwin has told thee what a ſacrifice
My heart hath made. Ambition, glory, pride,
And fierce reſentment bend beneath thy pow'r,
And yield the palm to all-ſubduing love.
Yes, thou haſt conquer'd. I am William's friend ;
The ſtruggle's paſt. I have perform'd the taſk
Aſſign'd, and come to claim my juſt reward.

   Matil. By virtuous acts the ſelf-approving mind
Is amply paid, nor ſeeks a recompence
From ought beſide. You have redeem'd your honour,
Turn'd to the paths of duty, and diſcharg'd
The debt you owe your country, and your king :
England and William will be grateful for it.
What can you wiſh for more ?

   Morc.   There is a prize,
More welcome far, beyond what e'er a king
Or kingdom can beſtow—thy love——

   Matil.   My lord !

   Morc. If to have ſav'd thee from the brutal rage
Of pitileſs ruffians ; if to have renounc'd
A victor's claim, and be myſelf the ſlave
Of her I conquer'd ; if to have releas'd
My bitt'reſt foe, becauſe ally'd to thee ;
If, after all my cruel wrongs, t' accept

The proud oppreſſor's hand, can merit ought,
I am not quite unworthy of the boon.

Matil. The good and juſt, my lord, demand our praiſe,
And gen'rous deeds will claim the tribute due,
The debt of humble gratitude; but love,
Love, that muſt mark the colour of our days
For good or ill, for happineſs or woe.
'Tis not the gift of fortune, or of fame,
Nor earn'd by merit, nor acquir'd by virtue,
All the rich treaſures, which, or wealth, or pow'r
Have to beſtow, can never purchaſe that
Which the free heart alone itſelf muſt give.

Morc. Give it with freedom then to him who moſt
Hath ſtudy'd to deſerve——

Matil. You talk, my lord,
As if the right of conqueſt cou'd beſtow
A right more precious, and a dearer claim;
But know, for now 'tis time to throw aſide
The veil that long hath hid from Morcar's eyes
The ſecret of my ſoul; and ſay at laſt
I never can be thine.

Morc. Ha! Never! O,
Recal that word!

Matil. I muſt not: Edwin knows
Thére is a bar of adamant between,
That muſt for ever part us.

Morc. Ha! for ever!
Diſtraction! can it be? Take heed, Matilda,
I am not to be mock'd thus. O, my brother!
Did'ſt thou not hear her? But aſtoniſhment
Has cloſ'd thy lips in ſilence——Never mine!
And wherefore not be mine? *(turning to Matilda.*

Matil. Becauſe I am
Another's——Well I know our hapleſs ſex,
So cuſtom wills, and arbitrary man,
Is taught in fearful ſilence to conceal The

The honeſt feelings of a tender heart :
Elſe, wherefore ſhou'd Matilda bluſh to own
A virtuous paſſion for the beſt of men ?
More. A virtuous paſſion! grant me patience, heav'n!
I am betray'd, abandon'd, loſt.   Another's!
Some fawning ſlave, ſome Norman plunderer,
Rich with the raviſh'd ſpoils of Engliſh valour,
Hath ſnar'd her eaſy heart, and tortur'd mine.
But I will drag him from his dark abode ;
Where e'er he lurks, he ſhall not 'ſcape my vengeance.
Thou hear'ſt her, Edwin.
  Edw.   Aye ! Who wou'd not wiſh
To hear the voice of nature, and of love,
Thus nobly pleading by the lips of truth ?
  More. Amazement! Thou art link'd with the vile'
That hath uſurp'd my right. All, all conſpire (ſlave
To make me wretched.
  Edw.   Why ſhou'd Morcar think
That lovely maid wou'd act beneath herſelf,
And make ſo mean a choice ? Now, on my ſoul,
I doubt not but the object of her love
Hath earn'd the glorious prize, and will be found
Deſerving of it.
  More.   Thou know'ſt him then ?
  Edw.   I do ;
Know him as brave, as noble as thyſelf :
One who wou'd ſcorn, howe'er the outward act
Might ſeem unworthy of him, to do ought
That ſhou'd diſgrace his family and name,
A man he is of yet untainted honour,
Of birth and valour equal to thy own,
Though fortune frowns upon him.
  More.   Now by heav'n,
But that I know thy eyes were never bleſt
With my Matilda's charms, I ſhou'd ſuſpect
Thou hadſt betray'd the ſacred truſt repos'd

In thy falfe heart, by unfufpecting friendfhip,
And wer't thyfelf the traitor.

Edw.   Think fo ftill.
Let fancy, ever bufy to torment
The jealous mind, alarm thee with the thought
Of feeing him whom thou haft thus revil'd;
Stand forth and dare the proof; fuppofe him here
Before thee, ready to affert his claim,
His prior right to all the joys that love
And fair Matilda can beftow: Then look
On me, and know thy rival in—thy brother.

Morc. Confufion! horror! mifery! O, heav'n!
Can'ft thou behold fuch complicated guilt,
Such unexampled perfidy, and yet
With-hold thy vengeance? Let thy light'nings blaft
The bafe betrayer! O, Matilda! falfe,
Deceitful, cruel woman!

Matil.   'Tis the lot
Of unprotected innocence to meet
The cruel cenfure, which to guilt alone
Is due.   I've not deceiv'd, I've not betray'd thee;
And wou'd'ft thou liften to the artlefs tale
I cou'd unfold———

Morc.   Away! I will not hear,
Nor fee, nor think of thee.   Deceitful villain!
Was this thy kind concern for Morcar's fafety?
Was it for this that fubtle Edwin came
A willing captive? Boafted William's ftrength,
And lur'd me to a bafe, inglorious peace?
That, like a midnight ruffian, he might fteal,
Unfeen and unfufpected on my love,
And rob me of Matilda.

Edw.   I abhor
A thought fo mean; the bare fufpicion ftains,
With fuch foul blot, my honour and my name,

I will.

I will not deign to anfwer thee. My birth
Alone might prove, to any fenfe but thine,
That I difdain it : 'Tis enough to fay
I am Earl Morcar's brother.

   More.   I difclaim
All ties of nature, or of friendfhip with thee,
And henceforth hold thee as my deadlieft foe :
As fuch I will purfue thee, flave, for know
Thou art my pris'ner ftill—Who waits there ? Seize
And guard this traitor———

             (Guards enter and feize on Edwin.
    MATILDA, *(kneeling to Morcar).*
             O, my lord ! if e'er
Soft pity touch'd thy breaft, if e'er thy heart
Felt the warm glow of fympathetic grief
For the unhappy, do not let the rage
Of thoughtlefs paffion urge thee to a deed
Of horror, which, too late, thou wilt repent.
O, fpare a guiltlefs brother, fpare thyfelf
The bitter pangs of fad remofe that foon
Shall harrow up thy foul, when radiant truth
Shall flafh conviction on thee. O ! forgive
And pity———

   Edw.   Rife, Matilda : 'Tis beneath
The dignity of innocence to kneel
Before proud guilt, and fupplicate a tyrant.
    MATILDA, *(rifing.)*
   I feel the juft reproach—Forgive me, Edwin ;
Henceforth I never will difgrace thy love,
By mean fubmiffion. Morcar, if thou hop'ft
For future peace, or pardon, fet us free.

   More. I'll hear no more, convey her to her tent.
   Matil. Edwin, adieu ! If honour, virtue, truth,
And mutual love, protect the innnocent,

                      We

We yet shall meet in happiness—farewel!

[*Exit Matilda guarded.*

Morc. Let none have entrance there, but faithful
    Siward.
Wou'd he were here, that I might pour my sorrows
Into his friendly bosom ! O, Siward !
Where art thou ?—Ha, he comes !

Enter SIWARD.

Siw.   My Lord, the troops,
Flush'd with their late success, refuse all terms
Of peace with William, and cry out for war
And vengeance———
Morc.   They shall have it. Now, by heav'n,
Thou bring'st me glorious tidings—well, what more ?
Siw. They have discover'd that the noble pris'ner,
Who had surrender'd, is thy brother Edwin ;
This hath alarm'd them ; they suspect you both
Of vile collusion, to betray their cause,
And yield them to the tyrant. If, they say,
You mean them fair, let Edwin be confin'd
And answer for the treason, with his life.
Morc. And so he shall : They cou'd not ask a boon
Which Morcar wou'd more readily bestow ;
Already their request is granted.—See
The traitor is secur'd. All-seeing heav'n !
Thou see'st how justice will o'ertake the wicked !
Siw. What can this mean ? Since last I saw my friend,
How the fair day that shone so bright upon us,
Is suddenly o'ercast.
Morc.   Alas, my Siward !
When thou shalt know—but 'tis enough to say
Matilda's false, and Edwin is—a villain.
                              Siw.

Siw. Amazement! can it be?

Morc. It is too true;
And I am loft for ever. O, Matilda!
Deceitful woman!

Siw. 'Tis not now a time
For idle plaints: Confult your fafety: Fly
This moment to the camp——your prefence there,
And that alone, may quell the rifing ftorm:
Leave Edwin to my care.

Morc. I go, my Siward,
Safe in thy friendfhip; I entruft to thee
My juft revenge. Yon mofs-grown tow'r that hangs
O'er the deep flood---'tis under thy command—
Place double guard—he muft not 'fcape--his fate
Shall be determin'd foon. What e'er it prove,
It cannot be more wretched than my own. [*Exit Mor.*

EDWIN, SIWARD.

EDWIN. *(pointing to the guards.)*
Where is my dungeon? My conductors here
Wait but your orders; give 'em their commiffion;
For you, it feems, Sir, are to execute
The friendly office: Do it, and be happy.

Siw. Guards, fet your prif'ner free—Thou little
know'ft
Of Siward's foul, to think it joys in ought
That gives another pain. I've learnt too well,
In fad affliction's hard, but wholefome fchool,
The leffon of humanity.

Edw. O gen'rous Siward, if thou haft a heart
To feel for others mis'ries, pity mine,
And poor Matilda's: She has not deferv'd
A fate like this.

C *Siw.*

Siw.   Alas! it rives my foul
To fee the tender bonds of amity
Thus torn afunder by the very means,
I fondly thought for ever wou'd unite them;
And the fair ftruâure, which my hopes had rais'd,
Of love and friendfhip, in a moment fhrunk
From its weak bafe, and bury'd all in ruin.
If thou can'ft prove thy innocence, as yet
I hope thou wilt, for in that noble mein
I read a confcious pride, that wou'd not ftoop
To ought that's bafe—Still may I hope to heal
Thefe bleeding woulds, and footh him to forgivenefs.
Mean time be free. Give me thy facred word,
The foldier's oath, thou wilt be found when e'er
I call upon thee; and yon tent alone
Shall be thy prifon; free to range around,
Far as my guard extends.

Edw.   Accept my thanks,
The humble tribute of a grateful heart;
'Tis all I have to give. The time may come
When Edwin fhall repay thee as he ought.

Siw. Is there ought more, which honour, and the duty
I owe my friend, permit me to beftow,
That thou wou'dft afk?

Edw.   O, grant me to behold
That injur'd maid, to take my laft farewel;
Then aâ as fate and Morcar fhall determine.
I give the pledge of fafety thou requir'ft,
And will be found—fpeak, wilt thou liften to me?

Siw. Of that we'll talk hereafter—come—within
I'll hear thy ftory—Thou but know'ft me yet
As Morcar's friend; hereafter thou may'ft find
I am ftill more the friend—of truth and virtue.

The End of the Third Aâ.

A C T IV.

SCENE, *An Apartment belonging to* SIWARD, *opening to a wood.*

EDWIN, MATILDA.

EDWIN.

THANKS to the noble Siward's gen'rous pity
For the diftrefs'd; once more we meet, Matilda,
But only meet, alas! to mourn our fate,
To feel each others woes, and to be wretched.

Matil. Eternal bleffings wait on him who thus
Cou'd fweeten forrow's bitter draught, and make
Captivity a bleffing! O, my Edwin!
A few fhort moments fpént with thofe we love,
Is worth an age of common life.

Edw,   With thee
Indeed it is; but we are on the verge
Of a dark precipice, and ev'ry ftep
Is dangerous. If Morcar fhou'd return,
And find us here together, we are loft
For ever; thou haft fcen, and fcen with horror,
The defp'rate rage of his tumultuous foul,
Let us avoid it, let us——

Matil.   What, my love?
Thou art my guide, protector, guardian, all
I have to boaft on earth. O! teach me where
To find fome bleft afylum for my woes,
And guide my footfteps to the paths of peace.

Edw. Let me entreat thee then——

C 2   *Matil.*

Matil.   O, speak! thou know'st
I have no will but thine.

Edw.   Then leave me, leave
This hated roof: I have a friend within,
Who shall conduct thee to the royal camp
In safety ; bear this signet to the king,
He will protect thee, and what ever fate
Decrees for me, Matilda may be happy.

Matil. O! never, never : Safety dwells with thee,
And thee alone. Without my faithful Edwin,
The peopled city, and the crouded court,
Wou'd be a defart to me. No, my love,   ꞏ
We will not part: The fame benignant pow'r
That led thee hither, that, beyond my hopes
Brought my loft Edwin to thefe arms again,
Will still protect that virtue which it loves.

Edw. Did'ft thou not tell me, that this very morn
Thou had'ft determin'd, as the only means
To shun my brother's love, on sudden flight ?

Matil. But then I shou'd have fled in search of thee.

Edw. Thou winning softness ! how shall I reward
Such unexampled tendꞏrnefs and truth !

Matil. By flying with me. Come, my love, lead on,
I'll follow thee to dangers and to death ;
Nor perils shall affright, nor labours tire,
When thou art with me.

Edw.   ꞏ   No : It must not be.

Matil. Why ? What shou'd keep thee here ?

Edw.   The ties of honour.

Matil. And are they ftronger than the bonds of love ?

Edw. To Siward's kind indulgence, well thou
         know'ft,
I owe this little interval of peace,
This tranfient gleam of happiness with thee ;
And shou'd I break my facred word, his life

                                 Might

Might anfwer for it; wou'd'ft thou have me thus
Repay his kindnefs ? No, my love; I may
Be wretched, but I cannot be ungrateful.

Matil Muft thou return then to that hateful prifon
When Morcar comes?

Edw.   I muft. O! think when I
Am pent within a loathfome dungeon, who
Shall fhelter then thy unprotected virtue ?
No Edwin there to fuccour thee : Who knows
What brutal luft and pow'r may dare to act,
On a deferted, beauteous, friendlefs woman ?
Diftracting thought! A monarch's vengeance then
Wou'd come too late ; wou'd make me poor amends
For my Matilda's violated charms.

Matil. He cannot be fo mean, fo bafe of foul,
Or if he fhou'd, I have a dagger here
To fave me from difhonour.

Edw.   What ! by death ?
Dreadful alternative ! O! hazard not
Thy precious life, but feize the lucky moment
Which fortune gives us, ere it be too late.

Matil. Urge me no more ; already I have felt,
Too deeply felt, the pangs of abfence from thee :
Another feparation wou'd be worfe
Than death, and all its terrors. No my love;
We are embark'd on a tumultuous fea,
And muft abide the fury of the ftorm.
The waves of angry fortune *may* o'erwhelm
But *fhall not* part us: We will.ftem the torrent,
Brave the proud ocean's rage, and gain the harbour
Of peace and happinefs—or *fink* together.

Edw. Thou haft foretold the tempeft, and behold
It rufhes on us.

        Enter

Enter MORCAR *and* HAROLD.

Matil. Ha! Earl Morcar here!

Morc. Harold, I thank thee; thy intelligence
Was but too true. (*turning to Edwin.*
Traitor! who fet thee free?
They wou'd have 'fcap'd my vengeance—falfe Matilda?
'Tis thus I am rewarded for my love,
My ill-tim'd mercy to a thanklefs brother.
Back to thy dungeon, flave. Guards, drag him hence,
To prifon, and to death. (*to the foldiers.*

Edw. Or death, or life,
Are equal to me, if I muft be torn
From my Matilda. But, whate'er thy purpofe,
Be fpeedy in thy vengeance, nor delay
The cruel work; for know, thy mafter comes,
William approaches—to revenge my caufe.

Morc. But not to fave thee.

Edw. Then farewel, Matilda,
Perhaps for ever—If we meet no more
Thou wilt remember—But I will not doubt
Thy honour, or thy love. I know thy truth.
Know thou wilt act as beft becomes thy fate,
Whate'er it be, and worthy of thyfelf.

Matil. Of *thee*, my Edwin, rather fay of *thee*.
Yes; I will copy well thy bright example;
I'll not difgrace thy love with woman's weaknefs,
But part without a tear. I will but ftay
To tell thy tyrant brother how I hate,
How I defpife him, and then follow thee.

Morc. I'll hear no more—begone!—away with him.
For thee, Matilda——— [*Exeunt guards with Ewin.*

Matil. What for me remains
I know too well; thy odious love, reproach
Unmerited, and threats which I defpife.

Thou

ถ

Thou think'ſt I have deceiv'd thee—think ſo ſtill.
Enjoy thy error.   Thou believ'ſt us guilty ;
'Twill make thee happy now—Perchance to find
Us innocent, may be thy puniſhment hereafter.

Morc. Aye, 'twas a proof of innocence to fly,
Thou and thy paramour together.

Matil.   No ;
I ſcorn a thought ſo mean. Cou'd I have left
My Edwin, long ere this I might have been
Beyond the reach of tyranny : beyond
Thy hated pow'r ; and ſafe beneath the wing
Of ſacred majeſty, in William's care.

Morc. In William's care !

Matil.   Thy conqueror's—for know
The hero comes—to ſcatter bleſſings round him,
To heal his country's wounds, chaſtiſe rebellion,
And puniſh falſe perfidious ſlaves like thee.

Morc. By heav'ns ! ſhe braves my wrath, inſults my
And triumphs o'er her ſlave.   (weakneſs,

Matil.   There was a time,
When with an eye of pity, I beheld
Thy hopeleſs love ; when I conceal'd my paſſion
For the dear idol of my heart, becauſe
I fear'd 'twould make thee wretched ; but thy rage,
Thy cruel treatment of a guiltleſs brother,
Has cancell'd all.

Morc.   Then, mark me : If thou hop'ſt.
For Edwin's freedom, ſhake off this vile paſſion ;
Yield thy proud heart to him who beſt deſerves it,
And meet me at-the altar—Two hours hence
I ſhall expect thee there—Beyond that time
He may not live to thank thee for thy bounty.

Matil. Then let him periſh—glut thy tyrant ſoul
With vengeance : bathe it in a brother's blood.
All ruffian, all barbarian, as thou art,

Thou can'st not murder his immortal fame:
Thou can'st not rob him of Matilda's love.
But know—when he, for whom alone this pulse
Wou'd wish to beat, this lazy blood to flow
Within my veins, when he shall be no more;
Another life shall satiate thy revenge;
Another victim shall attend thy triumph.

More. Thou talk'st it nobly —'tis the common trick,
The affectation of thy sex to boast
A fancied firmness, which ye never knew;
But with affrighted nature thou wou'd'st shrink
When death approaches.

Matil.   Put me to the proof.
If thou wou'd'st punish Edwin, know he lives
Within this breast—strike home, and pierce him there.

More. Imperious woman! thou defy'st my pow'r,
And let it crush thee.   If thy country bleeds
In ev'ry vein; if perjur'd Edwin falls,
As soon he shall, a victim to my rage;
Thou art the murd'rer; thou the parricide:
I stand absolv'd; the guilt is all thy own.

Matil. If it be guilt to suffer keen reproach,
Pain, persecution, terror, chains and death
For him I love, rather than stain my soul
With foul disloyalty, I am indeed
The guiltiest of my sex, and well deserve
The pangs I feel.

More.   Thou'st driv'n me to the pit
Of black despair, and I will drag thee down
To share the dreadful ruin thou hast made.

Matil. I know thy savage purpose; but remember,
The hour approaches when thou shalt repent
This base, unmanly triumph.   William comes:
Hear that and tremble, thou unnat'ral brother;
Nor rocks, nor caves shall hide thee from his vengeance;
                                        Inglorious

Inglorious and unpitied, fhalt thou fall,
And after ages fhall confign thy name
To endlefs fcorn, and infamy immortal. [*Exit Matilda.*

 Morc. Inexorable judge! I ftand condemn'd,
And fhall await my doom ; but not alone
Or unreveng'd fhall Morcar fall—henceforth
I bid adieu to love, and all his train
Of fond delufions—Vengeance! I am thine,
And thine alone :. Thou daughter of defpair!
Deftructive goddefs! come, poffefs my foul
With all thy terrors—Yes ; it fhall be fo.
A few fhort hours are all that niggard fate
Will deign to fpare me ; I'll employ 'em well,
For I will crowd into the narrow circle
A little age of mifery and horror:
Ha! Siward here! what brought thee hither ?

Enter SIWARD.

Siw.   Pity
For the diftrefs'd, I knew thou wert unhappy,
And came where duty call'd, to pour the balm
Of friendfhip in, and heal thy wounded heart.

 Morc. O, they have pierc'd too deep ; ev'n thou, my
Thou haft betray'd me : was it not unkind   (friend,
To fet my pris'ner free ; to let him meet
Matilda, and confpire againft my life ?

 Siw. Impoffible! by heav'n the artful ftory
He told, fo wrought upon my eafy foul,
I thought him innocent.

 Morc.   Haft thou not heard——

 Siw. From Harold only an imperfect tale,
So ftrange I cou'd not credit it.

 Morc.   Alas!
'Tis all too true : I am the verieft flave,

The

The meaneft wretch that e'er was trampled on
By an imperious woman: O, my friend!
My Siward! I have nought on earth but thee:
Shou'd'ft thou forfake me in this houf of terror!
But fure thou wilt not.

   Siw.　　　　　　　'No: Whate'er the will
Of wayward fortune may determine for us,
Behold *me* ready to partake thy fate.
If we muft fue for peace, let Siward bear
The olive for thee: if once more we caft
The defp'rate dye of battle, let me perifh
By Morcar's fide. Come, let us on together;
Shake off this load of unavailing forrow,
And feek the field; there, if we fall, we fall
With honour: if we rife, we rife to—glory.

   Morc. Talk not of glory to a wretch like me,
Bereft of ev'ry hope. There was a time
When that enliv'ning call wou'd have awak'd
My active fpirit, and this drooping heart
Bounded with joy; but my Matilda's loft:
Revenge alone———.

        (Enter a meffenger to Siward with letters.
   Siw.　　　　From Walfcoff thefe;
'Tis well—retire.　　　　　*[Exit meffenger.*
   (Reads)——How's this? then all is loft.
He writes me here, that William's fame in arms,
Spite of his cruel and oppreffive laws,
Hath rais'd him friends in ev'ry part: already
The northern rebels are difpers'd, and thoufands
Flock to the royal ftandard. To refift
Were madnefs.

   Morc.　　　And to yield were cowardice
More fhameful——

   Siw.　　　What muft we refolve on?
                      Morc.

Morc.   Death:
The wretches only hope, the wish'd-for end
Of ev'ry care, but I wou'd meet him cloath'd
In all his terrors, with his reeking spear,
Dipt in the blood of an ungrateful mistress;
And a false happy rival; then, my Siward,
Shalt thou behold me welcome the kind stroke,
And smile in agony.
    Siw.   Unhappy youth!
The storm beats hard upon thee; but our fate
Will soon be fixt, for William comes to-morrow.
    Morc. To-morrow! ha! then something must be done,
And quickly too. If William comes, he comes
To triumph over us: then, my Siward, who
Shall punish Edwin? who—shall wed Matilda?
I cannot bear it—If thou lov'st me, Siward;
For now I mean to try thy virtue;—swear
By all the pow'rs that wait on injur'd honour,
What e'er my anxious soul requests of thee,
Thou'lt not refuse it.
    Siw.   By the hallow'd flame
Of sacred friendship, that within this breast,
Since the first hour I seal'd thee for my own,
With unremitted ardor still hath glow'd,
I will not—Speak, my Morcar, here I swear
To aid thy purpose.
    Morc.   'Tis enough; and now
Come near and mark me: Thou command'st the tow'r
Where Edwin is confin'd.
    Siw.   I do.
    Morc.   Methinks
It were an easy task—you understand me——
Justice is slow, and—William comes to-morrow.
Thy friendly hand——
    Siw.   My lord!——
                            Morc.

Morc. Thou trembl'ſt — Well another time, my Siward,
We'll talk on't—ſhall we not? Thou mean'ſt to do
As thou haſt promis'd?

  Siw.   Certainly.

  Morc.   Then ſpeak,
And do not trifle with me.

  Siw.   Sure, my lord,
You cannot mean to——

  Morc.   Is he not a villain?

  Siw. I fear he may be ſo.

  Morc.   A hypocrite?

  Siw. He hath, perhaps, deceiv'd you, and deſerves—

 Morc. To periſh.

  Siw.   No; to ſuffer, not to die;
Or, if to periſh, not by Morcar's hand,
Or Siward's—O! 'tis horrible to ſhed
A brother's blood——

  Morc.   A rival's.

  Siw. Nature——

  Morc.   Love——

  Siw.   Humanity——

  Morc.   Matilda—

  Siw. (aſide.)   Gracious heav'n!
That paſſion thus ſhould root up ev'ry ſenſe
Of good and evil in the heart of man,
And change him to—a Monſter.

  Morc.   Hence! away,
And leave me—From this moment I will herd
With the wild ſavage in yon leafleſs deſart,
Nor truſt to friendſhip—but another hand——

  Siw. (muſing.) Ha! that alarms me—then it muſt be
And yet how far——   *(ſo;*

  Morc. You pauſe.

  Siw.   I am reſolv'd.

  Morc. On what?

               Siw.

Siw.　　　　To ferve, to honour, to—obey you.
Edwin fhall ne'er difturb thy peace again.

Morc. O glorious inftance of exalted friendfhip!
My other felf, my beft, my dear-lov'd Siward——
Confcience! thou bufy monitor, away
And leave me—Siward, when fhall it be done?
To night, my Siward, fhall it not?

Siw.　　　　　　Or never.

Morc. Let me but fee the proud Matilda weep;
Let me but hear the mufic of her groans
And fate my foul with vengeance—For the reft
'Tis equal all.　But tell me, Siward, fay,
How fhall I know the bloody moment? What,
Shall be the welcome fignal?

Siw.　　　　　　When thou hear'ft
The folemn curfeu found, conclude
The bufinefs done—Farewel. When I return
　With tears of joy thou fhalt my zeal commend,
　And own that Siward was indeed thy friend.

The End of the Fourth Act.

ACT

ACT V.

SCENE, *A Gothic Hall.*

MORCAR, HAROLD.

MORCAR.

TREASON and foul rebellion in my camp!
But I was born to be for ever wretched,
The sport of fortune.   These base mutineers————

Har. Your presence on the battlements, my lord,
Dispers'd 'em soon; they hang their heads in silence,
And all is peace.

      MORCAR, *(to himself.)*
                It is not so within.

Wou'd it were done or————

    Har.   What, my Lord?

    Morc.   No matter.

What urg'd my soldiers to rebel?

    Har.   'Tis thought
The gallant captive did by secret means
Excite them to revolt.

    Morc.   It must be so.
By heav'n thou mak'st me happy with the tidings:
His head shall pay the forfeit.

    Har.   Whilst he lives
We are not safe.

    Morc.   No more we are, good Harold;
'Tis fit he perish, is it not?   What say'st thou?

    Har. Prudence demands his life to save your own.

                        Morc.

Morc. O! thou haft given fuch comfort to my foul—
Har. My Lord——
Morc.   Be watchful : Bring me early notice
Of ev'ry motion : Go.   (*Exit Har.*
                         Or I muſt fall,
Or Edwin—Hence, ye vifionary fears ;
Ye vain chimeras, hence—It is no matter :
Confcience, I heed thee not ; 'tis felf-defence,
Nature's firſt law, and I muſt ſtand acquitted.
The prudent Siward feem'd to hefitate,
As if he wiſh'd, but knew not how to ſhun
The office. He who cou'd behold my tortures,
With all that cold tranquillity, wou'd ne'er
Have ventur'd to remove them. But I've truſted
The ſword of vengeance to a fafer hand.
What ho! Who waits ?
              Enter an OFFICER.
         That foldier whom thou faw'ſt
In private conf'rence with me, is he gone
As I directed him ?
    Offic.   My Lord, even now
I faw him haſt'ning tow'rd the tow'r.
    Morc.   'Tis well.
When he returns conduct him to me—Stay ;
If Siward comes this way, I'm not at leifure :
I will not fee him. (*ſtarts.*) Hark! did'ſt thou not hear
The folemn curfeu ?
    Offic.   No, my Lord.
    Morc.   Not hear it!
It ſhocks my foul with horror—Hark! again !
Hollow and dreadful! Sure thy faculties
Are all benumb'd.
    Offic.   Indeed, I heard it not.
Morc. Away, and leave me to myfelf,   (*Exit Offic.*
                              Methought

I heard a voice cry—ſtop—it is thy brother:
We lov'd each other well; our early years
Were ſpent in mutual happineſs together:
Matilda was not there—I do remember
One day, in ſportive mood, I raſhly plung'd
Into the rapid flood, which had well nigh
O'erwhelm'd me; when the brave, the gallant Edwin,
Ruſh'd in and ſav'd me—Shall I, in return,
Deſtroy my kind preſerver? Horrid thought!
Forbid it, heav'n! (*pauſes.*) I am myſelf again.
All pow'rful natuie! once more I am thine.
He ſhall not die—Who's there——

Enter an OFFICER.

My Oſwald! fly,
Fly to the tow'r this moment, haſte and ſave
My brother—Some baſe ruffian————
    Offic.   If, my Lord,
You mean the noble priſ'ner there, I fear
It is too late: This moment as I paſs'd
The citadel, I ſaw a mangled corſe
Drawn forth by Siward's order————
    Morc.   Slave, thou ly'ſt.
Away this moment, bring me better news
On peril of thy life.   [*Exit Offic.*
                          Who knows but heav'n,
In gracious pity, ſtill may interpoſe
And ſave me from the guilt? It is not done;
It *ſhall* not—*muſt* not be——All's quiet yet;
I have not heard the ſignal.   (*The bell tolls.*
                          Hark! he's dead:
My brother's dead—O! cover me, ye ſhades
Of everlaſting night! Hide, if ye can,
A murth'rer from himſelf. Ha! ſee he comes:

His

His wounds are bleeding ftill ; his angry eyes
Glare full upon me. Speak—what wou'd'ft thou have ?
Matilda fhall be thine : He fmiles and leave me——
      *   (*he paufes and recovers himfelf.*
'Twas but the error of my troubled foul.
O ! guilt, guilt, guilt !   (*throws himfelf down.*
          Here will I lay me down,
And end my days in bitternefs and anguifh.
          Enter SIWARD.
Who's there ? Ha ! Siward here.   (*rifes.*)
          Speak, murth'rer, fpeak,
Where is my brother ? Villain, thou haft fnar'd
My foul ; my honour's ftain'd, my fame deftroy'd,
And my fweet peace of mind is loft for ever.
  Siw. Matilda will reftore it.
  Morc.   Never, never.
The price of blood ! No : Cou'd Matilda bring
The vanquifh'd world, in dow'ry with her charms,
I wou'd not wed her. O ! cou'd I recal
One hafty moment, one rafh, cruel act——
But 'twas thy favage hand that——
  Siw.   I receiv'd
Your orders : 'Twas my duty to obey them.
  Morc. Where flept thy friendfhip then ? Thou
          know'ft defpair
And madnefs urg'd me to it——but for thee——
Thy callous heart had never felt the pangs,
The agonies of difappointed love ;
Thou did'ft not know Matilda—Curs'd obedience !
How often has thy infolence oppos'd
Thy mafter and thy prince ? how often dar'd
To thwart *my* will, and execute thy own :
But when I bade thee do a deed of horror,
And fhed a brother's blood—thou cou'd'ft obey me.
  Siw. Away ! this is the trick of felf-delufion,
                              The

The common cant of hypocrites, who rail
At others guilt, to mitigate their own?
I've been the mean, the fervile inftrument
Of thy bafe vengeance; but thou had'ft prepar'd
Another, a low ruffian, to perform
The bloody office; I deteft thee for it,
Defpife, abhor thee.

Morc.   Thou wert once my friend.

Siw. Henceforth I am thy foe—Thou haft deftroy'd
The beft of brothers, and the beft of men.

Morc. Defpis'd by Siward—then my cup of forrow
Is full, indeed—But this fhall———

(Attempts to kill himfelf, Siward wrefts the fword from him.

         Ha! difarm'd!

But coward guilt is weak as infancy;
It was not fo before I murder'd Edwin.

Siw. The murd'rer's punifhment fhou'd be to live,
And fhall be thine; thou know'ft not half thy guilt
Nor half thy forrows: I fhall rend thy foul.
Prepare thee for another deeper wound;
And know that Edwin lov'd thee, in his hand,
Whilft mine was lifted up for his deftruction,
I found this paper, 'tis the counterpart
Of one he had difpatch'd to William, read it
And tremble at thy complicated guilt.

    MORCAR, *(taking the paper)*
What's here? He pleads my pardon with the king,.
Afcribes my frantic zeal, in Edgar's caufe,
To ill-advis'd warmth, and recommends
His—murderer to mercy: Horrid thought!
I am the vileft, moft abandon'd flave
That e'er difgrac'd humanity—O, Siward!
If thou haft yet, among the dying embers
Of our long friendfhip, one remaining fpark
Of kind compaffion for the wretched Morcar,

             Lend

Lend me thy aid to fhake off the fad load
Of hated life that preffes fore upon me.

   Siw. Tho' thou'rt no longer worthy of my friendfhip,
Deaf to the cries of nature, and the voice
Of holy truth, that wou'd have council'd thee
To better deeds, yet hath my foolifh heart
Some pity for thee—After crimes like thefe,
There is but one way left—Say, wilt thou patient wait
Till I return ?

   Morc.   I will.

   Siw.   Remember, Morcar,
You promis'd me—I have a draught within,
Of wondrous pow'r, that in a moment lulls
The tortur'd foul to fweet forgetfulnefs
Of all its woes : I'll hafte and bring it thee,
'Twill give thee reft and peace.   *[Exit Siward.*

   Morc.   I hope for ever,
But where's the loft Matilda ? who fhall comfort
That dear unhappy maid, whom I have robb'd
Of ev'ry blifs.   O, fave me from the fight,
Ye pitying pow'rs !

             Enter MATILDA.

                She comes—diftraction !

   Matil.   O !
My lord, permit——

   Morc.   Away—I know thee not.

   Matil. Not know me ! 'tis the poor diftrefs'd Matilda,
Who comes to afk forgivenefs for the rage
Of frantic love ; the madnefs of defpair,
That urg'd me to fuch wrath and bitternefs
Of keen reproach ; but pardon—*(kneels.)*

                Gen'rous Morcar,
A woman's weaknefs : Speak and make me bleft.
Alas ! he hears me not.

   Morc.   Matilda, rife ;
I pray thee leave me—*(weeps.)*

                    Matil.

Matil.   Gracious heav'n ! he weeps;
Propitious omen! O, my lord! thofe tears
Are the foft marks of fympathizing woe,
And feem to fay, I fhall not plead in vain.

    Morc. Afk what thou wilt, for know, fo dear I hold
Matilda's happinefs, that, here I fwear,
If all the kingdoms of the peopled earth
Were mine to give, I'd lay them at her feet:
But much I fear they wou'd not make her happy.

    Matil. Alas! my lord, Matilda's happinefs   .
Is center'd all in one dear precious jewel ;
'Tis in *thy* keeping——Edwin———

    Morc.   What of him?

    Matil. Is innocent.

    Morc.   I know it.

    Matil.   Juft and good ;
He never meant to injure thee, indeed
He did not.

    Morc.   I believe it, for his nature
Was ever mild and gentle.

    Matil.   ⌐ Good, my lord,
You mock me.

    Morc.   No, Matilda; fpeak, go on,
And praife him : I cou'd talk to thee for ever
Of Edwin's virtues———

    Matil.   Then thou wou'd'ft not hurt
His precious life, thou wou'd'ft not———

    Morc.   ·   I wou'd give
A thoufand worlds to fave him.

    Matil.   Wou'd'ft thou? then
My pray'rs are heard, thou haft forgiv'n all,
And I am happy. Speak, is Edwin free?

    Morc. From ev'ry care—wou'd I were half fo bleft!

    Matil What mean you ? Ha! thy eyes are fixt with
            horror,
Thy looks are wild. What haft thou done? O! fpeak.

                                   Morc.

Morc. Matilda, if thou com'ft for Edwin's life,
It is too late—for Edwin is no more.
Matil. And is my Edwin flain ?
Morc.   Aye : Bafely murder'd.
O ! 'twas the vileft, moft unnat'ral deed
That e'er——
Matil.   Blafted be the cruel hand
That dealt the blow ! O, may his guilty heart
Ne'er tafte of balmy peace, or fweet repofe !
Morc. But ever, by the vulture confcience, torn ;
Bleed inward, ftill unpity'd, till he feek   .
For refuge in the grave.
Matil.   Nor find it there.
Morc. 'Tis well : Thy curfes are accomplifh'd all ;
I feel 'em here within—for know…'twas I.
I gave the fatal order, and my friend,
My Siward, has too faithfully perform'd it.
Matil. Siward ! impoffible ! There dwells not then
In human breaft, or truth or virtue—O !
Unnat'ral brother !—but I will be calm.
Morc. Alas ! thy fate is happinefs to mine ;
For thou art innocent.
Morc.   And foon, I hope,
To be rewarded for it. O ! my Edwin,
Matilda foon fhall follow thee—thou think'ft
I am unarm'd, deferted; doom'd like thee
To hated life ; but know, I have a friend,
A bofom-friend, and prompt, as thine, to enter
On any bloody fervice I command. *(Draws a dagger.*
Morc. Command it then for juftice, for revenge,
Behold ! my bofom rifes to the blow ;
Strike here, and end a wretched murd'rer——
Matil.   No ;
That were a mercy thou haft not deferv'd ;
I fhall not feek revenge in Morcar's death,
In mine thou fhalt be wretched——
(Attempts to ftab herfelf ; Morcar lays hold of the dagger.
                                   Morr.

Morc;   Stop, Matilda———
Stop thy rafh hand, the weight of Edwin's blood
Sits heavy on my heart.   O ! do not pierce it
With added guilt.

Matil.   No more, I muft be gone .
To meet my Edwin, who already chides
My ling'ring fteps, and beckons me away.

Morc. Yet hear me! O ! if penitence and pray'r,
If deep contrition, forrow and remorfe
Cou'd bring him back to thy defiring eyes,
O ! with what rapture wou'd I yield him now
To thee, Matilda---bear me witnefs---Ha!   *(ftarts.)*
'Tis he---Look up, dear injur'd maid---he comes
To claim my promife.

Matil.   It is, it is my Edwin!
(Enter Siward and Edwin : Edwin runs and
embraces Matilda.

Morc. O unexpeéted blifs ! what gracious hand——
Siw. Behold the cordial draught I promis'd you !
I knew thy noble nature, when the ftorm
Of paffion had fubfided, wou'd abhor
A deed fo impious—'Tis the only time
That Siward ever did deceive his friend.
Can'ft thou forgive ?

Morc.   Forgive thee ! O thou art
My guardian angel, fent by gracious heav'n
To fave me from perdition. O, my brother !
I blufh to ftand before thee—wilt thou take
From thefe polluted hands one precious gift ?
'Twill make thee full amends for all thy wrongs.
Accept her, and be happy.
(He joins the bands of Edwin and Matilda, then turning
to Siward)
That vile flave

Whom I employ'd——   *Siw.*

Siw.   I guefs'd his horrid purpofe,
Watch'd ev'ry ftep, and as the villain aim'd
His ponyard at the guiltlefs Edwin's breaft,
Turn'd fudden round, and plung'd it in his own.
The bloody corfe was dragg'd——

    Morc.   I know the reft.
O, Siward! from what weight of endlefs woe
Hath thy bleft hand preferv'd me!

    Edw. O, my Matilda! how fhall we repay
Our noble benefactor? Much I owe
To gallant Siward, but to Morcar more:
Thou gav'ft me life, but my kind, gen'rous brother
Enhanc'd the gift, and blefs'd me with Matilda.

    Matil. (to Morc.) Words are too poor to thank thee as
Accept this tribute of a grateful heart,   (I ought;
Thefe tears of joy; and, O! may ev'ry curfe
My frantic grief for Edwin pour'd upon thee,
Be chang'd to deareft bleffings on thy head!

    Morc. Alas! thy bleffings cannot reach me. Guilt
May plead for pardon, but can never boaft
A claim to happinefs: I only afk
A late forgivenefs. If a life of forrow,
And deep remorfe, can wafh my crimes away,
Let 'em be bury'd with me in oblivion,
And do not curfe the memory of— Morcar.

                     (turning to Edwin.
O, Edwin! fay, can'ft thou forgive the crime
Of frantic love, of madnefs and defpair?

    Edw. As in my lateft hour from heav'n I hope
Its kind indulgence for my errors paft,
Ev'n fo, my brother, from my foul I pardon
And pity thee.

    Morc.   Then I fhall die in peace.

    Edw. Talk not of death, my brother, thou muft live
To fee our happinefs complete, to hear

                             My

www.ingramcontent.com/pod-product-compliance
Lightning Source LLC
Chambersburg PA
CBHW020246090426
42735CB00010B/1857